```
                              087040
  797.1    Mohn, Peter B.
  MOH          Whitewater challenge
```

DATE DUE			
~~DEC 13~~			
~~OCT 26~~			
~~JAN 23~~			
~~OCT 19~~			
~~MAY 05~~			

OAK RIDGE SCHOOL LIBRARY

**OAK GROVE SCHOOL DISTRICT
EDUCATIONAL SERVICE CENTER
6578 Santa Teresa Blvd.
San Jose, CA 95119**

Whitewater Challenge

Whitewater Challenge

by Peter B. Mohn

Published by Crestwood House, Inc., Mankato, Minnesota 56001. Published simultaneously in Canada by J. M. Dent and Sons, Ltd. Library of Congress Catalog Card Number: **75-16085** International Standard Book Number: **0-913940-25-9** Text copyright © 1975 by Peter Mohn. Illustrations copyright © 1975 by Crestwood House, Inc. All rights reserved. No part of this book may be reproduced in any form without written permission from the publisher, except for brief passages included in a review. Printed in the United States of America.

Crestwood House, Inc., Mankato, Minnesota 56001

A kayaker with his eye on a big boulder just downstream. He's being watched by a group in the background.

PHOTOGRAPHIC CREDITS

Old Town Canoe, Old Town, Me.
  Cover, 3, 6, 8, 10, 15, 16, 18, 19, 20, 22, 26, 29, 31

Idaho Adventures, Inc., Salmon, Id. 27

Wisconsin Dept. of Natural Resources, Madison, Wi. 24

Minnesota Historical Society, St. Paul, Mn. 12

Whitewater Challenge

Just over one ledge, this paddler is moving quite fast toward another.

THUNK! went the slender red fiberglass kayak on the rock hidden under the river.

The kayaker worked furiously with his two-bladed paddle to get away from the rock. The kayak backed off a little.

Then the river's rushing current took the stern, or rear end, of the kayak and pushed it around so the boat was going sideways down the stream.

The paddler dug furiously again with the right blade of his paddle, trying to point his boat downstream again. With his last desperate stroke, he lost his balance and the kayak tipped over.

Everyone in the whitewater class tried to go through the gurgling rapids that day, but no one made it without capsizing.

All had experience in paddling a kayak on quiet lake water, but this was their first experience in whitewater, or the rapids of a river.

In time, and with practice, many would learn to do the "Eskimo Roll", a maneuver in which a kayaker, with one strong paddle stroke goes from upside down to right side up.

And in time, many would take canoe trips with families or friends in which they would paddle whitewater and quiet water.

Canoeing and kayaking are not the only two ways to have whitewater fun. People enjoy the mild whitewater in some rivers in inner tubes. Others go in special boats called dories. And others ride large rubber rafts in even the most turbulent rivers.

Whenever a river or stream goes downhill more rapidly than normal, we will find whitewater. A large amount of water rushing through a narrow canyon will cause turbulence.

There's that rock! An open canoe and its paddlers challenge some whitewater.

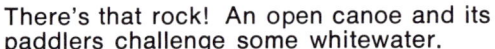

Whenever we are in whitewater, we can expect to find rocks. Rocks make it more interesting and more difficult.

The most extreme and dangerous whitewater is a waterfall. River riders usually carry their boats, or portage, around waterfalls and rapids which fall too quickly downhill.

Much whitewater, however, can be traveled in boats of one kind or another. Sometimes the sport is dangerous, but people who are ready for danger seldom have serious trouble.

People play in whitewater all over the world. They even race in mountain streams. Some race on a "slalom" course where they must go through the race course a certain way.

Many times, a slalom kayaker will have to paddle his boat upstream backwards because the "gate" next in line has been put there. Slalom kayaking and canoeing may be the hardest test for paddlers.

In the wilderness areas of Canada and the United States, a lot of whitewater can be found. The people who like to play in whitewater usually go to these places in the spring and early summer.

Spring and early summer paddling is better because the rivers can get low during the dry summer.

Both persons paddling on one side, this canoe is being aimed toward quieter water at right.

Everyone who has been on whitewater will tell you one thing. When your trip is over and your boats and paddles are put away you'll quickly forget all the calm water. And years later, the whitewater and the portages will still be strong in your memory.

Why is whitewater fun?

First of all it is part of nature. It looks dangerous, but it's something we can learn to do. And when we actually do it, we have accomplished something. Not everyone plays in whitewater, so we can do something special. That makes us different.

We can have good feelings about ourselves when we look back at a rapids and know that our strength and skill has brought us through safely. And if we are in a canoe with others, it can feel good to be part of a team.

Our rivers were highways for the explorers of the United States, so whitewater was an everyday thing for some of them. Going upstream, the explorers and fur traders often had to carry their heavy canoes and cargoes around the rapids. Coming downstream, they may have gone through, or "shot" the rapids.

Across the northern United States, men called voyageurs paddled long canoes in the fur trade. One canoe could have as many as ten paddlers.

The voyageur had to be rugged for the trips were long and some of the rivers were swift. But he also had to sing well, because they had to entertain themselves around their night-time campfires.

Going in to trade with the Indians for furs, the voyageurs carried "trade goods", beads, knives, kettles, traps and cloth. On their trips back, they carried furs.

SCUBA divers emerge from a northern Minnesota river with a collection of trade kettles lost by Voyageurs.

Not all of them made it through the whitewater. The Minnesota Historical Society has a collection of trade goods collected by SCUBA divers from some northern Minnesota rapids.

The goods were left there when voyageur canoes capsized more than 200 years ago!

The only people who have to go into whitewater now are the guides who we might hire to take us through. Very few people live so far away from cities and highways that they must shoot rapids for a living.

Most of us go to whitewater for the fun of it.

What do we need for whitewater fun?

Of course, we need a boat or float of some kind. We have to have a paddle—a single blade for most canoeing and a double blade for kayaking. Rafters and dorymen in the west may use long oars called "sweeps".

Some whitewater canoeists and kayakers wear helmets to protect themselves from rocks when they capsize. And everyone wears a lifejacket.

For whitewater kayaking, we may want to put "flotation bags" in our kayaks. The air-filled bags help keep the boat afloat and water out.

And if whitewater is only a part of a long canoe trip, we will have to bring food and other supplies along.

Many times, entire groups of canoeists and kayakers will take a trip at the same time. Being able to share the experiences is great fun.

How do we learn? The best way is in a group. Kayakers often learn to paddle, turn, and eskimo roll their boats in swimming pools. But the best way to learn about any adventure sport is to do a lot of it.

We may start with a class or a group, but it gets better when we can go "solo" — by ourselves.

Where is the whitewater?

Ready to kayak safely. These paddlers wear helmets and lifejackets. The "spray skirts" they have keep water from splashing into their boats.

Many states have maps of their rivers. Some maps even show where the rapids are. We can join a canoe or kayak club which may have favorite areas in which to play.

School and public libraries may have books on whitewater. Stores which sell canoes, kayaks and supplies also may have information.

In many wilderness and western canyon areas, we can find guides who do nothing but take groups of people into whitewater.

Whitewater people are careful people. If everything isn't just right, they make it right before they begin.

We should know our whitewater before we try it. If a state or a canoe club has rated the rapids we're going to paddle, we should know the rating in advance. Rapids are graded for difficulty from one to seven.

A Grade One rapids is easy. A Grade Seven rapids can be a killer. Our first whitewater trips probably should be in Grade One and Two rapids.

We don't rush into whitewater, either. If we're paddling some unknown rapids, the best way to go is to stop upstream, get out of the boat and "scout" the rapids from dry land.

The kayaker may be headed for the bottom of a sinkhole. These can be found in Grade Three and harder rapids.

Portaging around a rapids. This canoeist has a "pack" canoe, which is very light and easy to portage.

We may be able to see better ways of going through as we look at the rapids from land. Or we may, after scouting the rapids, decide to portage around this rapids and try the next whitewater downstream.

We want to be alive and paddling. The people who prepare for danger have fun. Those who don't can get hurt.

Once in the rapids, we have to do three things to stay upright and dry and get to the quiet water safely. They are:

1 — Don't hit rocks.
2 — Keep the boat pointed downstream.
3 — Keep the boat moving faster (or slower) than the current of the river.

How do we find an underwater rock?

In whitewater, there will be a number of V-shapes on the surface. Each V means there's a rock right

Two canoe campers in whitewater.

The bow paddler digs hard while the stern man steers hard, but this canoe is still in danger of upsetting on a large rock.

about at the point of the V. So we steer away from the points and aim for the "chutes" between the Vs.

The kayaker will see the V-shapes quite easily. But in a canoe, the person steering from the stern won't be able to see as well. The bow paddler must tell the stern paddler where to go.

Keeping the boat pointed downstream and going faster than the river current are closely related. If we don't paddle hard enough to go faster, the current takes over. With the river in control, our boat will quickly be turned sideways to the current.

And a boat turned sideways, or broached, can be bent double over a rock by the force of the current!

What happens if we capsize?

First of all, we get wet. On a hot summer day when all we are doing is playing, this is no problem. But if the capsize occurs on a trip of any length, we may be in trouble.

With experience, a kayaker might simply complete his eskimo roll and paddle off as if nothing had happened.

Fairly mild whitewater.

Canoeists may have to take their boat to a riverbank, haul it out and dump the water. A boat with water in it doesn't handle as well, so we should keep ours as dry as possible.

In the confusion of a capsize, things can get lost. Each paddler should be sure to stay with the boat, hold onto the paddle and remember what supplies were on the boat.

Above all, hold onto the paddle! It's no fun to be "up the creek" without one.

In cold weather take a change of dry clothing in a waterproof bag.

If we go canoeing and kayaking to stay dry, we go inner tubing to get wet.

If we see any whitewater at all, the rapids will be Grade One or Two at the most, and we might get a few bumps.

We should wear lifejackets when inner tubing, but most whitewater is shallow enough that we can touch bottom.

The usual clothing for an inner tube trip is a bathing suit and not much more. People who sunburn easily should wear a light shirt part of the time.

A tuber simply plunks into the middle of an inner tube and pushes off. Paddling is possible but not necessary.

Drifting downstream on Wisconsin's Apple River

The hottest part of the summer is best for tubing. Since the "boat" is round, it makes no difference which way we float downstream, head-first or toes-first.

A good tubing stream is a lot slower than a canoeing or kayaking stream, so the danger in the whitewater is less.

Many tubers go in large groups. They say it's much more fun that way. Some take soft drinks and picnic lunches with them. People talk, splash one another and watch for wildlife while tubing.

On some rivers, there are places to rent inner tubes. The people who rent the tubes also run buses which pick the tubers up downstream and take them back to the starting point.

On some of the great rivers of the west, people seem to risk their lives to travel on the whitewater of the deep canyons.

For many years, only a few tried to go through these turbulent waters. Now, guides take many people through every year.

Surfing is another form of whitewater kayaking, but it's hard to tell if this kayaker is getting ready to ride a wave or wipe out!

To begin a canyon whitewater trip, we may have to ride a horse or mule several miles down into the canyon. After loading the supplies into the rafts or dories, we push off.

The guide sets an example by buckling himself into a lifejacket. Spills can occur, even with a long rubber raft.

Instead of a paddle the guides use long oars, or sweeps, fastened to the raft by loops. These sweeps will give more control in the heavy whitewater.

Most raft trips through canyons begin in quiet water. The guide may begin by telling about the history of the area and what to expect. The scenery is beautiful. Canyon walls often glow with different soft colors.

"This is no fun", we might think as we drift aimlessly downstream. Chances are good the first stretch of whitewater is right around the bend.

All of a sudden, we're into it! Within a few yards, the river turns white and wild. The rubber raft bends and twists in more ways than we can imagine. Water pours over the raft from all sides. We get wet in an instant.

Running the Wild Sheep Rapids in Hell's Canyon of the Snake River. The rubber raft and its riders almost seem buried in whitewater.

The guide isn't playing around any more, straining against the long sweeps and keeping us away from rocks, other hazards and the canyon walls. With the raft bucking like a wild bronco we hang on tight.

At times, it seems like we're going uphill in this downhill river, riding a watery roller coaster which surges over unseen rocks underneath. Then, almost as suddenly as we got into the rapids, we drift out into quiet water.

The guide returns to a description of the river, the canyon and the next rapids. We feel the sun again, begin to dry out and bail water out of the raft. And so we drift, looking at the scenery, until the next rapids.

And that's what canyon trips are like — moments of sun-filled peace watching scenery and wildlife followed by frantic plunges in the surging current.

Shooting a chute. Both canoeists have their heads up, looking for the next obstacle.

Long before dark, our guides will stop on a sandbar and prepare the camp for the night. The canyons are so deep that the sun disappears behind their walls early in the afternoon.

Once ashore and dry, we'll discover just how tired the whitewater has made us. Not long after supper, the story telling will begin and we'll soon find the guide keeps the scariest campfire stories for last.

Whitewater is fun for those who know it. While we play in whitewater, we can also see wildlife — trees, animals and birds.

We know we are doing something that's good for us. We are closer to nature.

No matter how well we do in whitewater, we know we can do better, using the strength of our bodies and our skills.

Many families have grown up having whitewater fun.

Maybe yours can too.

One of the rewards of whitewater—a peaceful campsite in a scenic spot for the late afternoon and night.